Date: 7/27/12

Published by Creative Education
P.O. Box 227, Mankato, Minnesota 56002
Creative Education is an imprint of
The Creative Company
www.thecreativecompany.us

Design and production by The Design Lab
Art direction by Rita Marshall
Printed by Corporate Graphics in the
United States of America

Photographs by Alamy (blickwinkel), Dreamstime
(Ekaterina Pokrovsky, Nouubon), Getty Images (Tim
Chapman/Liaison, Hiroyuki Matsumoto, David
Muench), iStockphoto (Tom Delme, Eberhard Kraft,
Elizabeth Kratzig, Robert Linton, Diana Lundin, Viktor
Thaut, Clark Wheeler, Yuriy Zelenenkyy)

Library of Congress Cataloging-in-Publication Data
Riggs, Kate.
Alligators / by Kate Riggs.
p. cm. — (Amazing animals)
Summary: A basic exploration of the appearance,
behavior, and habitat of alligators, some of Earth's
largest reptiles. Also included is a story from folklore
explaining why alligators and dogs don't get along.
Includes bibliographical references and index.
ISBN 978-1-60818-104-9
1. Alligators—Juvenile literature. I. Title.
QL666.C925R54 2012
599.98'4—dc22   2010049122

CPSIA: 011212 PO1521

9 8 7 6 5 4 3 2

AMAZING ANIMALS

ALLIGATORS

BY KATE RIGGS

CREATIVE EDUCATION

Millions of alligators live in the U.S.

An alligator is a big reptile. There are two kinds of alligator. American alligators live in the southeastern United States. Chinese alligators live in China.

reptile   an animal that has scales and a body that is always as warm or as cold as the air around it

Some alligators are so dark green they look almost black

Alligators have thick, scaly skin all over their bodies. Their bodies are usually dark green or brown. Alligators look a lot like crocodiles. But alligators have wide, U-shaped **snouts**. Crocodiles' snouts look like the letter *v*.

snouts noses and mouths of some animals that stick out from their heads

Male American alligators

are about 13 feet (4 m) long. They weigh 800 pounds (363 kg). Females are smaller than males. Chinese alligators are much smaller than female American alligators. They are 5 feet (1.5 m) long and weigh about 90 pounds (41 kg).

American alligators are the largest reptiles in the U.S.

*Large birds called egrets
also live in swamps*

Alligators in the U.S. live in **swamps**. They also live in rivers and lakes. A lot of alligators are found in the states of Louisiana, Florida, and Georgia. Chinese alligators live along a river called the Yangtze (*YAHNG-see*).

swamps wet, muddy areas with a lot of plants

An alligator crushes a turtle's shell to eat it

Alligators eat meat.

Their favorite animals to eat are fish, frogs, and turtles. Sometimes they eat other animals near the water such as birds or small **mammals**.

mammals animals that have hair or fur and feed their babies with milk

Baby alligators are six to eight inches (15–20 cm) long

A mother alligator lays about 35 eggs at a time. She puts them in a nest and covers them with leaves and grasses. The babies **hatch** two months later. The baby alligators stay together in a group called a pod for almost two years. An alligator in the wild can live for 50 years!

hatch come out of an egg

Most alligators live alone. Some smaller alligators live closer together. Alligators like to spend time in the sun during cooler parts of the day. When they get too hot, they go back into the water.

An alligator spends a lot of time in an area called a gator hole

Alligators spend a lot of time floating in the water. They even sleep while they float! An alligator swims by moving its tail back and forth. On land, alligators can run on their toes.

Young alligators sometimes ride on their mothers' backs

Today, some people go to Florida to see alligators in the wild. Other people visit alligator parks or zoos to see them. It is exciting to get close to these big reptiles!

Alligators at parks and zoos perform for food

An Alligator Story

Why do alligators and dogs not get along? People in Louisiana used to tell a story about this. There was a mighty alligator that lived in a swamp. Everyone respected him except the neighborhood dogs. One day, a dog tricked Alligator into leaving the swamp and eating food at the house of his owner. When the people saw Alligator in their house, they chased him back to the swamp! Alligators have disliked dogs ever since.

Read More

Johnson, Jinny. *Alligator*. North Mankato, Minn.: Smart Apple Media, 2007.

Simon, Seymour. *Crocodiles & Alligators*. New York: HarperCollins, 2001.

Web Sites

Enchanted Learning: Alligators
http://www.enchantedlearning.com/subjects/reptiles/alligator/coloring.shtml
This site has alligator facts and a picture to color.

National Geographic Kids Creature Feature: American Alligators
http://kids.nationalgeographic.com/kids/animals/creaturefeature/american-alligator/
This site has pictures and videos of American alligators.